W9-AOJ-189

THE

POETRY

OF

WICKEDNESS

and

other

poems

FOR NED
I. L. Y. W. & P., B. G.
AND FOR CZESLAW
PREEMINENTLY NOT OF THE DEVIL'S PARTY

THE
POETRY
OF
WICKEDNESS

and

other

poems

by

LYN
COFFIN

ITHACA  HOUSE

Poems in this collection have been published or accepted for publication by the following periodicals: *Concerning Poetry, Northeast Review, Literary Review, Dakotah Territory, Aspen Leaves, Aspen Anthology, Paunch, Ball State University Forum, Poet Lore, New Orleans Review, Descant, Hollins Critic, Kansas Quarterly, Wind,* and *Green River Review.*

The publication of this book is made possible in part with funds from the Tompkins County United Arts Fund and with public funds from the New York State Council on the Arts.

ITHACA HOUSE
108 N. Plain St.
Ithaca, New York 14850

Distributed by Ithaca House and by Small Press Distribution, Inc., 1784 Shattuck Ave., Berkeley, CA 94709.

Copyright 1981, by Ithaca House

Library of Congress Cataloging in Publication Data

Coffin, Lyn.
    The poetry of wickedness and other poems.

    I. Title.
PS3553.038P6   811'.54   81-20085
ISBN 0-87886-116-5   AACR2

TABLE OF CONTENTS

PART ONE

PART TWO

PART THREE

PART FOUR

PART ONE

INHERITANCE

Grandfathers are always dying. Mine
Had strokes in Florida, cancer of
The throat in Michigan. He tried to whine
But pipes in his neck like parts of a stove
Turned his smallest whisper to a boom.
He scorned the striped pajamas he got as gifts,
Complained about the loud curtains in his room.
He mocked doctors and nurses alike, and sniffed
Suspiciously at us. He chuckled when
He made me cry. Up to the last, he harped
On all my faults, and tried his best to din
It into me that I was dumb; he carped
About my every move. And yet his dying
Testament was that he'd always loved me most.

The poker-handed dead are good at prying;
His boring eyes are humorless, opaque.
I do the bidding of my unbidden guest—
He powers dreams and shatters me awake.

MOTEL AUBADE

The blanket presses its woolly chest
on the nervous sheet that doesn't know
what to do and so just lies there.
It likes seeing what's under it,
Everywhere: the sun only eggs it on.
And the pillows lie in each other's
plump, middle-aged, self-satisfied arms,
like two cooks surprising each other
into a fling after an evening spent
bowling. I understand now: your matches
lie open on the bedside table: an
assembly line of blue-collar men—
small, but tough—lusting after cigarettes,
the statuesque girls in the seminary next door.
I understand: you really didn't use me—
I wasn't used last night. It was only these
Things—sheet, blanket, cigarettes,
pillows, matches—they outnumber us. And
we were their way of getting to each other.
Your digital clock blinks voyeuristically.

PAGANINI REBORN AS A WOMAN POET

. . .he was accused of maintaining an
alliance with the Devil himself, thought
by many to stand at Paganini's right
elbow to assist his wizardous bowing
arm.
—Joseph Scuro

The devil—who looks a bit like a child
Psychiatrist—(He wears vested suits
In subdued plaids and soft glossy-brown
Italian shoes which show off his small narrow
Feet to best advantage)—signed a contract with
Me, or I, with him. (As with any good
Mind-doctor, it wasn't easy to tell who
Was doing what to whom.) But I know this contract
Lies at the bottom of everything these days,
Locked, like future-minded pirates' bullion
In a metal chest at the bottom of
What used to be a sea but is now a lake,
Still vexed with tides, though untroubled by salt.
If you stand on the single dock this lake
Affords, you can look down through bright water
And catch a glimpse of the brighter chest, like
A glint of something in the devil's eye when
He hands you the mirror you asked to play with,
Where the reflection is so perfect you feel
As though you were looking down into a
Made-to-order lake of glass which calls out
To you like the calmest, most motherly

3

Of mothers . . . Which not so much summons as
Invites you to be your eye-round, eye-gray stone
Self, invites you to fall into your first
Bed and be at rest forever . . . This
Contract is why your cupboards are stocked
With food, your mailbox with personal notes,
Submissions accepted, checks made out to you,
Why your bed comes complete with a tall, dark
Stranger who wants to be your husband if
You want him to, and doesn't if you don't,
Who only invades upon request and is
Ready to retreat at a moment's notice.
This contract is why your face stays as smooth
And inscrutable as that of a wheat-haired young
Girl you wish were your daughter who leans out
Over bright water, and you absolutely
Can't tell whether she's afraid— Can't tell even
As she jumps whether she jumps because she
Wants to jump, or because she so very much
Doesn't. As smooth as that of a girl who only
Looked the same, who stands forever on a round
Table, center of a circle of bearded
Men who make her spin around so fast, she gets
Dizzy, and falls. Whereupon they laugh, pull down
Her underpants so the one who looks like
Her father, the doctor, the devil, can
Poke fun at her with one enormous finger.
Whereupon she decides that though she knows
Who that man is, she doesn't and will never
Willingly know what he is doing, or to whom.
She only dimly understands that she

Is on her back, looking up as from
The bottom of a lake. Like the crab
She saw her father catch, the same one she saw
The next day, lying in an uncovered fish-keeper
Between the posts at the end of the dock—
The day she started acting funny,
The day she overheard her mother say
That unknown Someones had poisoned the lake
With factory-made chemicals because
They were set on doing the devil's business.

HALFWAY BETWEEN DROWNINGS

The ice on the pond is getting thin.
The first spring is not the real spring
But the flowers don't know that—they
Respond despite themselves— Little girls
Coming grudgingly forward in the slowest
Of magnetisms toward the candy a stranger
Extends. The minor character
In all of this—the pond—recollects itself
Like a spellbinder halfway between drownings . . .
The old wolf is already on unsteady legs when
He slips into the paddock—among the magnificat
Of bleating. He is like a knife that tests
Rising dough. Bringing him here, his instincts
Have carried him beyond intention, but
The sheep don't know that—don't, in fact,
Know anything—and are properly terrified.
The wolf dies with his lank tongue lolling
In a wolfish grin that makes a "Q" of his mouth.
And the small flowers like grade school show-offs,
Keep coming backwardly forward toward
The candy-handfuls of a one-eyed strangler.

TO YOU, AGAIN

With hands like scholars, you unearthed
The snow-banked book that gave my age,
Unbound it with a lover's laugh
So glacial drifts slid off the page.
Nothing shames but shame itself,
I'm clothed in body, liquid as day.
And when we run, my hair streams back,
Flows like rivers, waves away
The last three thousand miles. Just look!
The smiles, the kiss you'll never plant
Take seed in breath and space.
And spring their blooms like roses
In the graveyards of my face.

THE DAYS OF THE WEEK

A kind of scarecrow, here I stand.
A bird starts to circle and soon I see
A big black bird perched on either hand.
Another bird comes and eventually
Seven birds have settled in a humpy row
Along the edge of me.
I start to shake and away they fly,
Looking for another scarecrow
Steadier than I.
Those seven birds are gone and still
The farmer has stones, and birds to kill.

HOSPITAL POEM

Loud voices in the corridor. I wonder
Who but not what— One thing I've learned is not
To ask wrong questions . . . There's wooden thunder
At the door. The doctor enters, not
Smiling. And how are we today? I match him
Eye for eye. He trots out learned terms like
Dappled greys. I try to look as though I'm
Listening, but any voice is lost on me.
The sounds I'm open to are of a different
Kind, the frosty sounds of operations.
Metal tables covered with thin sheets
Are wheeled through corridors where nurses settle
Everybody's hash . . . It feels so good
To give up newer ghosts and let them roll me
Back through smiles like hoops, cucumber smiles,
Until I'm back in the saddle again.
The farm is not the same, though. I remember
Scattered grain uncounted chickens fluttered
Over, golden in the dust. Now somebody's
Guernsey has her hind foot in the churn—
She's knocked the milk pail, brained the lapping cat—
Her udder's gone all thumbs like woolen mittens;
I wonder who will drown the dead cat's kittens.

TO YEVTUSHENKO, NAME ENOUGH

Hey, Yev, you Roosian rooster, cocky at the cracking dawn,
Bantam bully and precocious pecker (all your bright red plumes),
Just when I had you figured for domestic fowl, you metamorphose:
You head a storm of ducks, come scudding wild-eyed over all my
    marsh,
And make my hunters, decoys, and my seasoned dogs, burst
    inward
Like a dream and disappear. My mind's still fitful gusts can test
    themselves
Against the freshly-laundered trousers on your private line.
    Weathered
To the geniality of elders, they have moved with winds yet proved
Unflappable. Sometimes, you are as true, as sternly whimsical as
    oceans,
Linking arms with opposite and rocky shores. Sometimes, you
    clang and
Boom—narrow-tongued and partisan: an old, slope-shouldered
    bell.

MEDEA MOM

Mother, sitting bolt upright on your
Rickety old redwood chaise longue, do you know
There's no pillow under you any more?
Do you remember how, when father finally
Came out from behind his desk and plumped himself
Down on that pretty, plastic pillow
One hot afternoon last week, he made it
Spill its curly, sheepish insides on the grass?
I think you do: I think you think it makes you
Seem starker, look more intense, to sit—and now,
Recline, pillowless on the rope webbing.
Perhaps you even hope the webbing will
Slip from its moorings all of a sudden—
Letting you down, not at all gently:
Then you could tell everyone again about
Your brittle, aristocratic bones . . . Would-be
Medea mom, you stare blackly up at
The noon sun, counting on me to be
Watching you from somewhere in the shade.
And I am watching you, from safe inside
The house my father's money
Bought at your insistence, because
"Shore property values always go up."
I stand here next to the jalousies,
Watching you through slits . . . You are waiting for me
To apologize . . . But I will never
Apologize—not if you get burned to a
Crisp, turn redder than your redwood chaise.
Just minutes ago, you were flirting with

11

My mild, academic boyfriend,
Pretending his real name was Clark Kent, saying
He offered you a refreshing change from
Listening to your husband, the executive,
Talk business all the time. Then you asked my friend
How it was that I had managed to corral
Him. Well, mom, I managed because I'm as flexible
As a snake, as supple as a rope that's been forced to
Weave a pattern, a self-sustaining web of itself,
Between two redwood arms that were always
Outstretched, as if in an effort to fend things
Off . . . And now, even if—even *when*—that red,
Wooden frame collapses, the rope webbing
Will maintain the adaptable weave of
Itself: It can be fitted to another frame.

IN THE STUDY, JUST BEFORE LUNCH

Ben Jonson's too tall for the third shelf:
I raise him to the second but now he comes
Before St. John. I lay him on his side but
His spine and Spenser's rush past each other
Like express trains and he presses on Stevens
Like last night's dinner. I shrug and thrust
Him into a crowd of convivial Cavaliers. Then
I notice Whitman and Wilbur—bearded jowl by
Downy cheek. I see that Frost is boxed in by
His own Major Themes and that if I extract
The critics like teeth, he'll be one foot into
Murder in the Cathedral. Murmuring "Metaphoric
Fences," I accept the status quo as provisional
And leave the room imagining me, Coffin,
A slice of something between Chaucer's rye and Hart
Crane's sesame-seeded delicatessen bun.

PART TWO

UNWRAPPED GIFTS

for A. B.

When her husband was alive, he had liked
Surprising her with small bottles of scent
Or handkerchiefs embroidered in the corners
With tiny clusters of flowers or, once,
Silly-looking angels blowing trumpets.
He never wrapped such gifts. It was a kind of
Joke they shared: he would extend one large,
Weather-reddened fist toward her, and she
Would take a long time prying it open,
Shyly peeling back his strong fingers until
The tiny bottle or the linen flowers
Stood revealed. But now her husband is laid out
In a box whose top will not even be made
Until tomorrow. And she lies upstairs,
Tossing and turning on the bed they shared,
Almost as if to prove to herself that he
Is the one the Lord saw fit to take and not
She herself. In her mind's eye she sees
A cellar (Before this, it was always
Attics and spinning wheels she saw)— She sees
A cellar, their cellar, but without a trace
Of dust or any sign of damp. To the left
Are the wooden cellar steps, just as he
Built them—twelve in all, all twelve swept clean.
And on the topmost step, lit from above and
Beyond by the gently swaying kitchen light,
Sits a round red apple. Even as she watches,

The apple wobbles. It makes a schoolgirl's
Hesitant somersault to the step below.
The next somersault is bold—the next,
Precipitous. And now the only comfort comes
From knowing nothing can be done . . . Down and down
The apple throws itself, not faster, but
Slower and slower—it seems to stop without
Stopping . . . And then it hits the floor, hits
Bottom—lands against the stones and breaks white,
Breaks open all at once, breaks out of itself . . .

For all that day, (her not-quite-yet-a-dream
Keeps telling her), that apple has been lying—
A real apple in a real cellar, next to
The staved wooden barrel her husband made.
That barrel holds hundreds of apples which were
Her husband's continual delight—
He used to say that owning an orchard,
However small, made up for having to live
So close to the railroad tracks . . . Last year at
This time, he would have hoisted the barrel,
Carried it easily up the cellar's
Twelve steps, and have set it in the pantry.
When guests came, he would take his apples two by
Two into the parlor, offering them to
Visitors— Holding the apples out in his
Strong clean hands, challenging the guests to find
A single flaw or bruise, a single break in their
Ruddy skins. Turning each in his hand like an untraveled globe.

FINE DISTINCTIONS

for E. H. C.

You skip past this poem like whatever I can think of that skips—
A stone, a rope, the child of foreign parents
On your light-years way home from parks where giggling bullies
Missed you by inches. You've established yourself by now—
You're an evader of bullies, and anything thrown
In your direction—button-eyed bears, milk bottles,
Black piano-keys that wiggled loose, like teeth,
Paper airplanes, potato chips borrowed
From tomorrow's picnic, flowers with fancy names.
You skip past this poem—past a man with filmy eyes
And a bed that lowers itself from the side of his room
Like a horse that is tired of rearing (or a drawbridge in
The wall of metaphor)— An empty room, this:
Full of dust that swarms with almost instinctual life,
A room where light falls through the window like
An impressionable young lady with strange ideas
Of etiquette, caught in a comfortable swoon.
Were he still here, the artist who moved out
Would certainly uncork the wine his girl-friend
So foolishly abandoned when she fled,
Muttering about men in general, artists
In particular, and holding an orange hankie
Like a carrot in front of her own adorable nose.
As it is, the artist's non-detachable hangers
Swing their bony hips forlornly in
The closet like—like a string of hookers
Whose pimp's been shot. And his black suitcase, hinges

18

Gone, gapes up at them with an old derelict's
Weathered air of semi-phonographic
Self-absorption. Now your hand has grazed
The door-knob: the spherical cold doesn't make you stop—
It only makes you stop skipping. Wrapping
The chilled hand in the other like a green
Bottle in a waiter's cloth, you proceed with greater
Gravity to greener pastures— Down the hall,
First door on the left, across from the b. r.—
The home of the homely English lady of whom
Even your mother approves because *She don't keep*
Liquor or soft drinks where kids can get at them . . .

Soon I'll follow you down the hall, down the long
Corridor. Listen— Don't you hear, in
The bathroom, tap-water running? And,
Under that, like river-stones—someone,
(Me) seating himself on the rim of
The empty tub as though contemplating
A backward dive onto porcelain?

NOW'S THE TIME

I'm powerless in the face of my own violence.
I have only to see a plate-glass window and my fist
Insists on traveling through it in a slow silent film
Of blood— Thin ribbons trekking up my arm,
And with what roseate perversity!
They're trickier, extend a more formal
Invitation to return to sources than
Bullet-headed salmon pushing upward—
Weaving around the small inverted tussocks,
The introjected muzzles, of drinking cows,
Who, at the slippery advent, raise their heads—
Afraid to swallow . . . So there I am, my fist
The latest furniture in a furniture-showroom
Window. There I am, and now's the time
For you to leave me . . . Go, friend. Trot past me
Up the crowded street, with unlowered head,
Sporting a garland on each milky horn.

THE DEATH OF ALLEN GINSBERG

Luckily, the Secret Police came in.
Allen perked right up.
Everybody's glass was empty so he held aloft a giant wooden
    pepper-mill and read aloud the first twelve pages of
    a verse salute to different kinds of solidarity he'd
    just written on the bottom of a Kleenex box.
I felt duty-bound to take the so-called Prefect of Police
    aside.
"You're not the fuzz at all," I pointed out.
He nudged me with his wings. "Allen would be disappointed
    if he knew," he said. "Besides, we are a force for law
    and order!"
Then they surrounded him (It seemed so damn official!)
    and wrapped him in some kind of Indian gauze.
Allen fixed us with his chrysalid eyes and started drifting
    upward.
From on high, hovering among the Romanesque arches, he
    spoke:

WAITRESSES OF THE WORLD,
KEEP YOUR BALLS ABOUT YOU.

At last he was allowed to disappear.

21

THE DIME-STORE FISH

It is difficult to say what I am, or
Tell what happened to me. I was spawned
In a large, colorless world that tasted more
Like metal than manna. It soon dawned
On me: the close-knit net of death was my
Only out. The time came. I was glad to feel
Taken up out of all knowing . . . I
Came to my senses to find heaven was real,
Marvelous. I was there: with a few others,
I drifted peacefully through this land
Of coral and crystal. But one of my brothers
Stiffened: the net came down. I can't understand.
Even here in heaven, it seems, death descends.
What happens to those for whom heaven ends?

CROSSING THE BRIDGE

I stand in grandmother's kitchen and look at the picture
Painted on a Sunday plate. At the center
Of the stunning Chinese sunshine, the blue wall
On the far hill looks impossibly good, breathtakingly
Appropriate. And something else— I see
Those men with hats like arrowheads, those mandarin men,
Pushing a red wheelbarrow over the bridge
At the heart of the white-as-an-apple sunshine.
And in the center of that red commotion
Is a flicker of chickens, about as many chickens
As grandmother used to keep. Then, across
The blue-veined perfection of that eggshell wall, across
That eastern construct, something extends itself,
Come into its own. I have no doubt it's grandmother's
Wisteria . . . Her trailing Georgia blooms deserve
Their place of honor on that arched blue barrier.
The summer evening smoke of their fragrance
Establishes sunshine and marching men, colors
That vision of chickens and bridge, and makes it this,
Makes it what I see . . . I stand in grandmother's kitchen,
Lost in the picture painted on her Sunday plates.

GOOD FRIDAY, GOING HUNGRY

What should we do, said the trembling boy, the cold
Child curled as a hand against the cold
Spring drafts as around a flame—the child gifted
With strong desires, his face small but gifted
Too, with a pinch, as of salt, of something needed,
Something borrowed from a neighbor. His eyes needed
Belief to make them beautiful— They'd been hard,
Been old from the beginning— They were raisins, a hard
Sweetness, as he found himself in his empty plate:
His brother and sister had taught him to make each plate
A mirror, to see his own face rise like a cold
Sun beyond the trees painted in its center.
The three made a circle at the table, its center
On the other side of childhood from me—a dark
Round of promises and secrets, dark
Vows made in the shadow of cellar doors.
I, thinking fond gestures could open doors
Between us, kissed him on the back of his neck—
Bent like that, in that backwater room, his neck
Was the stubborn neck of prayer, though veins in his wrist
Preached sermons of hunger and the hand that stemmed
    from that wrist
Held a knife as if it could, in another life,
Have been a wand and God summoned to life
At moments of our choosing, not his. The looks
Of children speak volumes, speak lives of their own, and
    the looks
Of these, being glass slivers, being birds, being blue
Arrows, sailed to the heart of childhood, to the blue

Regions, the country where the sacred is kept like a promise.
But I, the stranger whose mangled sounds seemed to promise
Blood, who entered their world of eggshell tissue
Like a giant thumb—I shared bone, blood and tissue
With all three, yet knew our kinship held no answer
Fit for them. None of my answers was the answer
They craved. I stood a moment in the blue heat
Of their flickering regard, touched by the white heat
Of fingers twined like tendrils around stainless steel.
I turned away without asking, my ribs a steel
Cage for an iron bird . . . Lambs at the table—
You bend your heads, but your hours are curled like the fists
Of roses, your silence drums like rain, like fists
On a chest as hard and dry as mine. Your silence
Cries to me—Mother— But mothers must turn from the silence,
Extinguish the sight of empty plates, the knowledge
That sits at the cold-water heart of the oldest morning
—Of sacrifice, repeated mindlessly.

THE NOTE

Propped against my blue, Oriental sugar bowl
Is a note—black words spoiling the creamy surface:
I leave it there and flee into the snowy street.
Defying the green-eyed parental judgments,
The jealous recriminations of red-eyed
Traffic lights, I make my way boldly
Between snow-covered cars, wolves in sheep's clothing.
I spend three hours at the farmers market,
Cooing over ruddy infants and russet
Apples, warily touching precocious
Christmas trees, as insistent upon their own
Spiny integrity as starfish, or
Old maids . . . At what I guess to be high noon,
I walk slowly down to the river, filling
My jacket-pockets with round, heavy stones.
But there is no bridge where I remember it,
And the river itself is so shallow,
A drowner would have to be horizontal.
So I walk back home, leaving behind me
A trail of round, heavy stones—like a modern
Gretel, a Gretel in reverse. Now that
The stones are gone, I can hear once again
His keys, my keys, the keys I reclaimed last night,
This morning, making their own witless music . . .
So I make my way back to him—I open
The door and the still-yellow kitchen dawns on me.
I see a note parked against my Oriental
Bowl like an unwanted invitation,
An invitation to someone else's wedding:

"I can't live like this," it says. I take the smooth
Wide steps to the bedroom two at a time
And the keys in my pocket make disapproving
Sounds like my mother when confronted with my
Single bed, more like the smug little click
A full suitcase makes when closing . . . I pause
Dramatically in the doorway, but
I don't catch him, as I think I will,
With his hands wrist-deep in the top dresser drawer
Or zipping the side-pockets of his hard blue
Suitcase . . . So then I look down, open my fist,
Uncrumple that white paper: "I can't live
Like this," it persists in saying. What can't be
More than moments passes in concentration—
The keys in my pocket growing as heavy
As stones, I recognize the writing, the scrawl,
The message as my own . . .

AN AMERICAN POET GOES ABROAD

circa 1920

New York sits like a three-legged cart at
The corner, heaped with huge apples and hoping
To be enormously upset. Summer here
Is a brass reproduction of Whistler's
Mom, dead as a lion-flanked door.
Who wants to be one of the flies struggling
In or out of this large red Gogolian
Buttoneer? No one. So let's do it,
Let's go. "Go and let go," as Jesus
Said. Or maybe it was Oscar Wilde.

Even without the poetry, evening falls.
The central sound is of the boot never dropped—
One hobnailed boot thuds upright, thuds
Upright on the narrowest board in the room,
The floorboard running closest to his side of
The bed, a maple four-poster where his parents
Obligingly died two years ago, one after the other,
As regular as clockwork. His thirty-year-old
Bride, who has been married to him half her life, lies
Rigid and waiting. Standing high over the bed in the
Not-quite darkness, he is granted a vision, given
An over-view of his own geography; he even seems to see
Beneath the homespun surface of things: It comes to him
In a rush— This quilted bed, this patchwork farm—
Their meager swells hide bones and boulders that
Begrudge not *him* so much as what he does,
How he requires them to behave:
The shale outcroppings, the muddy waterhole,
Fences that threaten to unravel the land,
Unravel *him*, like thread . . . But it, she, isn't
Strong enough to deny him: day and night
They toil at each other. So it is now:
His heavy mounting of the stairs has told her
More than she wished to know, has told her
This would happen: his weight, his drunkenness,
His hard, unmindful thrust toward generation.
The square, knotted-leather jacket-buttons
She had sent for and sewn on with doubled thread
Press against the length of her spine with a ready-made

Precision. And everywhere a button presses,
A barb of bone presses back in the only
Kind of answer she can make, and *feel* that she
Makes . . . His jeans are still on, though unbelted:
She thinks she can tell the exact spot where
His zipper comes apart like train tracks: each rail
Riding the incline of each buttock.
She is glad he is this drunk: he is
Just something that has to ease itself like
Hot weather. But the wet cold boot pressing hard against
Her cold dry shin bothers her . . . He makes her
Wear dresses, she remembers— He wants his friends to see
What good legs she has on her, he says— Thin, not like
Their cow-wives have. It's a good thing for her, he says,
She never let herself go to seed . . .
It's true enough her legs are thin and straight
And so white they look like they've been dusted with
Some kind of powder—that new fertilizer he bought, maybe.
Once, when she was sitting in the tub, legs and arms
Stretched out in front of her, she had the oddest notion:
Her skin and *her* had somehow been reversed, she thought;
What people saw of her was just what people
Shouldn't see, shouldn't want to see—her limbs, for example,
Her legs and arms, were like riverbeds in times
Of drought, when wires buzzed alive with heat and
Watering holes were eyeless sockets . . .

And now, of course, thanks to the boot
There would be a public bruise. It would bloom and flourish—
It would turn purple, orange, violet, green—
A strange, hothouse flower would grow, would spread,

Would lavish itself on the chalky soil
Of her skin . . . *Her skin.* And if anyone came to
The house, anyone at all, they would see it,
They would see the bruise he had given her—
The tropical flower their love had brought forth.

PART THREE

THE DEATH FROG

He makes dark bargains with his garbled eyes,
Admits to being something of a bungler.
"Grab it," he says. "Grab it. Grab it. Grab
It." The muscles in his throat bulk large
As though he'd swallowed something by mistake.
He hunkers in old leaves. You put the hand
Without the basket down— He sprockets out
Like crazy parts in cartoon engines. You feel
Silly to feel scared. You tell yourself that
Frogs aren't really cold and fetid. *Think high and
Dry*, you say. But can't shake some links: under-done
Alligators— Jowly uncles— Puffy snakes.
That chill's expected: you take the wrong tone;
At night, this real unmagic frog turns to stone.

RIDERLESS HORSES

He stood on the shore in a circle of ruins
Recalling the words of the lady in white:
"If you manage to waylay the magical children
As they ride to the ocean through their ominous country
And make certain your lips never touch any salt
The secret they tell you will save you from drowning . . ."
He dreaded the thought that he might die by drowning,
He began to revise his view of the ruins.
He scraped a stone tablet encrusted with salt
And discovered words that were filled in with white:
"Here lies the king of an alien country,
Challenged and murdered by magical children."
As the shadows grew long in the land of the children,
He doubted the words that might save him from drowning:
He remembered tales that were told of this country,
That Satan had made of God's city these ruins,
Turned the moon clumsy, a crony in white,
And scattered stars on the night sky like salt.
He kept himself steady by thinking of salt—
Suddenly he was surrounded by children
Weaving a circle of pale gold and white.
Then he grew unafraid and forgot about drowning.
Now as he stood in the center of ruins,
He looked like a king from an alien country.
"Children, I've come to your perilous country,
Where the moon's like a stone and the stones are like salt
To learn why you ride to the sea through these ruins."
Clearer than water came the words of the children:
"Tomorrow's the day set for trial by drowning."

35

They brought him a mantle—vermilion and white,
Led the way to the shore where a woman in white
Pronounced him the king of the magical country
And prepared him for dawn, for the trial by drowning . . .

He strode through the water, lips flagrant with salt,
And they followed as one, the woman and children,
Leaving riderless horses to stray through the ruins.

For the woman in white and the magical children,
Drownings are doors: They returned to their ruins.
But the man was left settled in the country of salt.

IN MEMORY OF ROETHKE

That day seemed ready-made as a suit,
The nondescript suit from respectable ranks
A gangster wears when he goes public.
Everything seemed its own monument,
As if at a party the deep voice of a prankster
Who hid behind potted palms had said,
"Nobody move, I've got you covered."
The time was poised like the egg of a rooster
On the peak of a roof in a children's riddle.

He made mint juleps in a yellow kitchen
On Bainbridge Island: he noted the map—
Put his finger on where he was.
A trick of sighting turned the island into
The small, big-gilled fish it wanted to be, and
It swam off . . . He ambled back outside,
Leaving the juleps to cool in the pantry
While he had a swim . . . He took his dive,
Swam to the children's end—

And the three ladies every poet knows
Were there to lift him out of the water,
His face as bland and noncommittal
As the water, as the sky.

THE ASPEN POEMS

Salt

Crystals;
The taste of my skin;
A mouth as wide as oceans;
Deep and bitter as anyone's blood.

Desire

for Neil

All my dreams are
Now giraffian—awkward,
On an imaged plain. Slowly,
It dawns on me—the sun insinuates
Itself around my morning's eastern
Edge, unfolds itself in Oriental fanfare;
My hands behave like chastened nuns.

Milk

Matron of the monotone,
Thick as faith and dull as rest.
Moth-like mouths of mindless babes—
Ice-floes swell a blue-veined breast.

Rumpled cows with fabled flanks,
Suns of butter, clouds of cream,
Copious horns and melted moos—

I'm awake, as up as sky
But sunk knee-deep in dream.

To Terry

My tongue once flew like tilting birds
Over your salty, poignant skin.
Now like a half-crazed fox it flattens itself
Against the back of a baffling cave.

THE WOOD AND THE WATCH

The first prison was built around a large
Courtyard and they used that yard to stack
Siberian timber: the whole area
Was, to use the Americanism,
Under-developed, and lumber was its
Only resource. We prisoners existed
To cut lumber, but so many of us
(I don't mean to be facetious, just truthful)
Were so busy dying, we didn't have
Much—what's the idiom?—heart for the job.
They conferred and decided upon
A Socialistic Competition. So,
I said. And what if I refuse to enter
The lists? Simple, they said. Then you don't eat.
The morning came as it always does,
Even in prison, and we began:
I had a short, rough axe that suited me
And red woolen mittens, a child's mittens
Because of my small hands. I worked like—not
Like a maniac, as you would say— like an
Automaton. Lunchtime came and went
And still I worked. When it grew too dark to see,
They made me stop. It was more comfortable
For them that way . . . Another time, another
Courtyard, another prison—Archangelsk,
I think—we, just off the train, were camping
In the courtyard, doing whatever it is
Prisoners mostly do— It isn't waiting,
Exactly, though it looks like it. Anyway,

One of us must have gotten too close
To the wire: a guard shot him, climbed down from
His observation tower, turned the man
Over, as a bureaucrat turns over
A form, a piece of paper—checked his neck
For signs of life, found none. That would have been
It, except the prisoner's watch caught his
Attention. He lifted the watch hand to his
Ear, and listened. What he heard must have been
Satisfactory, because he took the watch.

RETAIL OUTLETS

Birth was a matter of cutting costs.
My mother gave birth like other women
Spend money, and vice versa. My father
Was like the store he managed from time
To time: one window might say Coming
Soon, the other pronounced the enterprise
Closed. I couldn't have pets as a girl—
Their upkeep was high—so I bought a begonia
Greener than money. It sponsored one flower,
One Grand Opening, then it proceeded
To fold. I think I came of age
When I looked back at the cushioned chair
In which I'd been reading marketing manuals,
And saw my chair still gaping after me
Like an entrepreneur with a leathery mouth
And his pawnshop mind on retail outlets.

Now that I'm married, there's time to wonder:
Do other husbands tell their wives—
Attend to business, watch the overhead?

MIRROR WOMEN

I

Her hands are soft,
As soft as mouths or bandages;
Like butterflies in a paper month;
Like a moon surprised
By an early sky.
She moves like a shepherd-girl,
Blurry with dreams,
Through herds dark
With remembered sleep.

II

There are flourishes here,
Here in this everyday squared-away
House. She stands at the door
Shaking crumbs from a cloth;
The dog lies perfectly still
On the mat where the key is hidden,
And the bricks are steady
With their own obedient fire.

43

STONE WINE

And we'll all drink stone wine
When Johnny comes marching home...

He weaves his way home—one large, weather-reddened
Hand trailing an empty bottle. When he gets to
The place where the trees close in on him,
He is a brigadier again. Thus,
The empty bottle becomes a cane and
He is on assignment in Africa
Or India—batting away the swarming
Arms of the dusky little buggers who
Try to embarrass and impede him . . . By the time
He has climbed the front steps and entered
The glassed-in front porch, he no longer holds
His bottle by the neck: he grasps the base
Firmly in his left hand and opens the inner
Door, liking the feel of the brass doorknob in
One hand, the glass bottle in the other—the round
Balance of those two cold, smooth things. He walks
With not at all comic stealth across
The carpeted hallway and opens the door
Under the stairs, the door to what she
Always insists upon calling "the guest
Bathroom." He doesn't fumble for the light
As usual, but points his glass rifle
Where he knows the toilet to be cowering
Like a yellow-bellied gook. "Halt!" he cries. "Halt!
Who goes there? Who's doing what in my bathroom?"
Now he nods at the dark, shadowy sea below

44

Him, the unblooded hordes who speak to him
From the round dark mouths of guns: first in silence,
Then in a roar, then in the darkness which is
Both, and before . . . He tosses the bottle
In the wastebasket, his memory a high flare
In whose light the hand-grenade explodes, but
Turns out to be nothing more patriotic
Than a firecracker at a children's party . . .
He turns and climbs the stairs, not remembering past drills,
Past exercises where he had been made to climb—
Remembering nothing, he does as he's been
Taught— Because the doing must be all, must be
Everything. Otherwise . . . Otherwise, you have
. . . The woman . . . She will be lying in bed,
A clock and a glass at her elbow, a book
Open in her hands. She will be on the edge
Of a circle of soft light, in a nightdress
That shows everything. She will say she has been
Waiting. He will nod . . . Despite himself, he will answer and
Say: "Those who wait are empty."

WHEN I WAS CRAZY

When I was crazy, a psychiatrist
Had me look at drawings to find out what
Was wrong with them. He insisted,
So I locked my eyes on each black-and-white square. But
There was one whose fault I couldn't make myself make out—
A winter landscape where everything fit:
Tracks across the snow, the receding back
Of a small, dark man, circling birds. I finally quit
Looking, admitted I couldn't find a mistake.
The doctor made a large black
Mark on his sheet. "There are two errors in that one,"
He said. "You should note, first, that the picture lacks
Shadows despite the clean winter day, the sun
Low in the sky. Secondly, the man's tracks
Start in mid-snow . . ." I could hardly sit
Still: I felt my irregular heart contract
To something like a knot of intricate
Daring, that nothing could distress. There,
In the exact spot where others drifted
To cold conclusions, someone had made a start.

FROGS AND BABIES

Can this be healthy or even normal—
To think of frogs and babies in the same breath?
Green frogs, blue babies— Surely froggy green
And baby blue don't do whatever it is
Colors are supposed to
To each other. I never was too strong
On colors or connections
But I used to think I knew about cookies.
I used to think the cookie Alice ate
Came packaged in a box marked
I suppose I'm going crazy.
That proved incorrect, however.
The box says nothing about anything.
It concentrates on being reassuring,
Squares its shoulders and does its job,
The job of setting tables like good examples.
The paper smiles in a general, cardboard way
And tries to look typical. But forget all that—
Think of it as a party if you like,
A party you don't have to go to.
Someone furnishes a crackerbox house:
You Come as you are and Bring your own.
In my case, I come as a frog. I bring a
Botched-up baby and ladle him into various arms.

47

PART FOUR

BEDTIME

Good night, (child's name)
How we hate to see you go...
Good night, (child's name)
Gee but we will miss you so.
But we'll all be waiting for you,
(Child's name), while you roam.
Good night, (child's name)
Don't forget to come back home.
* —Family Bedtime Song*

You tried to breathe but the world kept closing
Your eyes. Bedtime did it, when
Darkness was like your father's hand
Whittling away clean edges because he said
They were dangerous. Being so collared,
Suddenly your legs went out from under you,
Your feet bicycled fast, churning the air
Like boats turning the dark lake-water
To foam, or when the warm black lady in
The kitchen swooshed all her white skirts at you . . .
But you knew black was black and white, white in the
Daytime. Feet were down, and water. Air was up.
So when you were held upside down over
The white square bathtub or the dark square bed,
It seemed more than possible you would soon
Find yourself at the wrong end of laughter
Like a telescope, again see yourself
Get caught holding the stiff rectangle
Called a menu upside down. It seemed likely

50

You would soon be squirreling upside down
In the dark, like the forgetful, buck-toothed Squee
Who always forgot where he'd stashed his nuts.
Perhaps you would eat your way through the crust, then
Have to swallow Midway flames when you got to
The center . . . You almost *felt* yourself begin
To spiral downward through the ground, like water
Leaving the white, inverted bosom of
The basin for the long, tunneling dark which
Sooner or later would mean China—would mean
Being rightside up in a country where
Rightside up was upside down, a place where
People looked at you crosswise like not-quite
Sleeping yellow dogs who lay in the sun
Scratching themselves absent-mindedly
While you were told to let sleeping dogs lie;
And where clothing must be worn inside out
So you could see labels at the back
Of everyone's neck, labels written in
Chinese, a way of writing that seemed to have
No o's, no zeroes, no circles—nothing
That looked the same upside down and thus
Provided excuses for not knowing
Which way was up . . . Suspended, pedaling
Air like a bicycle too big to ride
And tasting dirt, grit, pieces of someone's
Driveway, you consider crying. And of course
That dark warm kitchen woman reaches out
Her arms to you, wanting to embrace you
Like the dark lake water behind the boat
Does to every line of boy-tracing foam.

51

You understand she wants only to hug
And not hurt you; you also realize
She's too large to maintain any such small
Distinction for long. You hesitate as if
For the dive you're only allowed to practice:
Teeth like toes grab the edge of the end of
The dock, and then you start the long glide toward
Cover— Now you want the dark to gather you in,
To swallow you up . . . And yes, of course
At the very last you will close your eyes—
Lost, as at sea, in your knowledge that
The whole round world is trying not to breathe.

FLOATING WOMEN

Beyond the boats that nod beside the concrete
Wharf like sleepy children nodding over tales
Too old for them— On the water that tenders its bright
Blue sway within the bestial hug of the rocks,
Women are floating.
As upright as swans, as buoys, their white skirts bloom
Above the water like fallen clouds, like rafts.
I will swim to the center of that breasted cloud, those swans,
I will cling to the nearest skirts, fearing otherwise
The bitter gargle of salt.

RECOGNIZING THE SOUND

The other patients called him Mr. Too Song
Or Mr. Tong Soon. I asked about him:
"He's a manic depressive," said a patient,
Harold, a manic depressive himself.
Harold said in the "bad old days" before
I arrived, whenever the shrinks in
Morning session asked Mr. Soon how he was,
He'd say "Top of the World, Top of the World," and
Then immediately rush out of the room,
Down the hall, to the bolted-from-the-outside
Door. He would stand and pound on the door until
His tiny fists were red, whereupon he would
Burst into tears, cry "Comme il faut!" and vanish
Into his room. "It wouldn't have been so bad,"
Harold added, "but he has a bad heart— He
Was sent here direct from the *real* hospital."
In the lounge before my first morning session
I asked Mr. Song where he was from. Many
Patients had asked that, Harold said, and gotten
No response. But— "Vietnam," he said right away.
"I come from the country of Vietnam." And
In morning session, after he'd said, "Top of
The World," he stole a look at me and stayed in
His seat . . .
                Later that day, Denise arrived.
From then on, I didn't exist for anyone
But Harold— Certainly not for Mr. Soon
Or myself. I watched helplessly as
The tiny couple began to revolve around each other

54

Like the porcelain figures on a glass-domed music box.
Now he spoke only to her: he asked her how
She'd gotten where she was. She looked up and down
His five-foot frame with her beautiful, frightened eyes.
"Through the front door," she said in French. He smiled.
"I can see the top of your head," he replied in the same
Language. "Your part is very straight." And she smiled
Tentatively back . . . "Made for each other,
Tiny, foreign, and probably both of them
Filthy rich," Harold said as we followed them
Around the garden during exercise hour.
The wall was too high for either of them
To see anything but sky on the other
Side, but Mr. Tong said he'd often walked there
"In my former life, comme il faut," and he
Described the scene to her: the East River Drive
Was just beyond the wall, beyond that was
A strip of green and a lovely narrow path;
Then came the wide river itself. She asked
If the rushing sound she heard was the river:
And he, who must have known better, who must
Have remembered all the cars, said it was.

By making a strenuous effort, it was
Possible for each of us to think we
Could keep up our peaceful circling,
Could walk in our walled-in garden forever.
Still, when Denise heard on the evening news
That a hurricane was headed for New York,
She turned uneasily to Mr. Soon—
"Will it hit the clinic, do you think?"

55

He took her tiny hand in his: "Not at all,
My dear," he told her. "The clinic is private
Property." And perhaps because, as always,
He spoke to her in French, as always what he
Had to say seemed to me to make perfect sense.

The next day, Denise was gone—sucked up by what
Harold called "The vacuum cleaner of the
Big outdoors." I went to Mr. Song's room:
And found him standing next to the bed, staring
At where the window would have been. "Here we are,"
I said in English. "Here we are together
At the Top of the World." And had the almost
Satisfaction of seeing him rush past me
Into the hall . . . Seconds later, down the long
Corridor, there came to me as I
Lay on his bed, the sound of a strong but
Muffled beating, as of a perfectly normal heart.

THE FOX VITA

Ars longa, vita brevis—which is why,
Quick brown fox that I am, I've skipped
Past the farmer's lazy bowser and slipped
Into this whitewashed little coop
Where the farmer's wife always neatly tucks
Five or six of her plump white
Chickens like folded papers in an envelope.
Eyes accustomed to the dark, I see three
Mouthwatering feathered poems on either side of me.
Memories of fox disturb their poultry sleep—
The ones that survive to dream tonight
Will dream of teeth . . . And here am I, Mr. Sly,
Dependent on a covey of uncertain clucks
Too dumb to tell if the eggs they feel are
Under them or in them . . . Well, Ars longa,
Etcetera, especially if you happen to be
A roosting toothsome pullet in my vicinity.

THE DUEL

Early morning madness: stars like wind-up toys
Betray quite separate confusions—they whirl
Like toothless gears. Below, two figures start
Weaving through the shivered silk-and-shadow gray
Of groping branches, parting a sea of snow
With their knees . . . The bullets begin stoically, stay
Self-possessed until the finish: then they show
Other colors, unburden themselves like boys
Whose dreams of release speak straight to the heart
Of the purest, most innocent girl.

NUMBS

Grandmother lay sick, slowly dying of
Something called a stroke, which meant she often
Switched the words on things and asked for a comb
When she wanted a book or the blanket.
She told my mother while I was downstairs
Practicing scales with a six-year-old's
dedication,
"That child makes points." Mother said this almost
Ungarbled statement was a good sign for
Both of us. Yet a few days later,
Grandmother was dead in her sunny room whose
Long windowsill boasted an enormous
Red geranium in a small clay pot . . .
When grandmother finally died, mother was out
Shopping, the nurse was nowhere to be found—
And left me. Grandmother began to ask for
What sounded like "Numbs," a word the dentist used
in ways that scared me. I tried bringing her
Things that had worked in the past—magazines,
Books, a comb, a brush, cold cream, another
Blanket, though it was sunny and warm. But
Grandmother kept saying "Numbs . . . Numbs . . ." in her
Insective voice. As soon as she was quiet,
I knew she was dead . . . At the funeral, I
Found time to wonder where grandmother had gone
And if she'd found there whatever it was
She wanted . . . Such questions disappeared with
My seventh birthday and second grade, but still—
I've hated the smell of geraniums for

43 59

Seventy-seven years, and it only
Occurred to me today, when I was buying
White crysanthemums for my great-granddaughter's
Room, that perhaps what grandmother wanted
Was to smell that red geranium— Perhaps
That was the reason the geranium was
The one portable thing I didn't try.

COLORS LIKE SPOKANE

Ignore all the colors that look like Spokane.
Cut through the dangers of brown, the seductive
Enrollments of blue— Sneer back at red and
Reduce it to ribbons by shouting this sentence:
"This hurts me more than it does you."
Address grey through a megaphone— Use an
Interpreter, a title if you own one. Be bland
With the yellow— Think recipes. Be unsparing
Of the pink. Say, "Mommy's little baby's going
Down the tubes." Triumph over fields of purple
Like a stork with scissor legs . . . Talk of
Community projects until you reach green.
Cast it down, denounce it—
Not kindly, either, as you would
A disease, but with the aluminum tones of political
Agendas . . . Before the adult role hardens, revert.
Now you're a seventh-grader at a dance. Say, "First to
Come and last to be chosen. Yah Yah Yah . . ."
When the green turns into a rubber ball,
Refuse to kick it. Say, "Say after me,
I hate games." If a fat girl emerges from the woods
Like rubber cement, roll her up from the bottom,
Call her your Imponderable if
You want her. Don't if you don't. If you do,
Your hands will be strange, will be slick with green
And the woods will be full of foxes.

61

A LIFE

That's more like it, I finally heard him say.
    I'd do without the forceps if I could.
As I relaxed, I felt the world give way.

At ten, I slipped out after dark to play.
    Father didn't hit me, though he thought he should.
That's more like it, I finally heard him say.

At twenty, I had a stage lover. I lay
    Trembling in his arms in a cardboard wood.
As I relaxed, I felt the world give way.

We married. For ten years, he managed to stay
    Faithful. When he transgressed, I said I understood.
That's more like it, I finally heard him say.

At forty, beds got blanketed with gray.
    I wanted to die gracefully if I could.
As I relaxed, I felt the world give way.

I dream of God, discover I can pray,
    Can be obedient for my own good.
That's more like it, I finally hear him say.
As I relax, I feel the world give way.

EIGHT WEEKS AFTER HER DEATH

He stood by the door in the same place she'd always stood
At such times, brushing the snow from someone's hood.
But these guests hadn't known her. He hung someone's coat,
Took them all on a tour, gave them time to note
The public things—the slate floor she had walked
As if walking on water . . . They were all careful to talk.
He tried to listen but the living room plants caught
His attention, the extravagant begonias she had taught,
She had *coaxed* into growing inward. Tomorrow he would turn
Their crimson blossoms toward the glass. They could learn
What that felt like . . . He was short of breath:
He concentrated on his childhood girl-friend Beth
Who had dug with him toward China and shared the feeling
That people there must walk like flies on the ceiling.